Original title:
Whirlwind Wishes

Copyright © 2024 Creative Arts Management OÜ
All rights reserved.

Author: Maya Livingston
ISBN HARDBACK: 978-9916-90-548-7
ISBN PAPERBACK: 978-9916-90-549-4

Winds of Transformation

Whispers carried on the breeze,
Change is looming, hearts at ease.
Leaves turn golden, dance in flight,
Opening doors to new delights.

Old paths fade, new roads unfold,
Stories waiting to be told.
With each gust, the soul takes flight,
Embracing dawn, releasing night.

Clouds dissolve into clear skies,
In the transformation, wisdom lies.
Nature's canvas, bold and grand,
Painting growth across the land.

Threads of Destiny

Woven tightly, paths entwine,
Moments crafted, by design.
Choices echo in the night,
Guiding dreams towards the light.

Fate's tapestry, rich and vast,
Each thread pulled from the past.
Weaving futures, hopes align,
In the fabric, hearts combine.

With every stitch, a story told,
In the weft, our dreams unfold.
Together, we shall find our way,
Threads of destiny hold sway.

Tailwinds of the Heart

In whispers low, the breezes swoon,
They lift the heart, like songs of June.
A gentle push, a swift embrace,
Guiding dreams in open space.

With every pulse, a current flows,
Through winding paths, where comfort grows.
The skies above paint tales anew,
With tailwinds strong, we'll dare pursue.

Tornadic Tales

Winds collide in a swirling dance,
Caught in the storm, we take our chance.
With hearts aflame, we ride the gusts,
In shattered skies, we place our trust.

The thunder roars, the lightning strikes,
Every soul feels the wild spikes.
In chaos found, our stories blend,
Tornadic tales that never end.

Dervish of Delight

Spinning round in a joyful whirl,
A dance of colors, hearts unfurl.
Each laugh a note, a melody sweet,
In the dervish's grace, our worlds meet.

With every twirl, the worries fade,
In a tapestry, we're lovingly laid.
Joy's embrace, our spirits ignite,
Under the spell of delight's light.

Surges of Imagination

From quiet thoughts, ideas arise,
Like waves that crash beneath bright skies.
Infinite realms, where dreams take flight,
In every surge, we seek the light.

A canvas vast, with colors bold,
Stories written, adventures told.
Through boundless seas, our minds will roam,
In surges of thought, we find our home.

Flurries of Ambition

Dreams dance softly in the night,
Chasing shadows, caught in light.
Each step forward, a whispered call,
As hopes and fears begin to sprawl.

In the silence, ambitions rise,
Like winter flurries 'neath dark skies.
With every heartbeat, steadfast beat,
We summon strength, refusing defeat.

Paths unfold, though uncertain still,
Guided by the fire of will.
In these moments, we embrace,
The challenge we're destined to face.

So let the flurries swirl and play,
In the heart of night and day.
For every snowflake tells a tale,
Of dreams that flourish and prevail.

Ribbons of Fate

Woven threads in a tapestry,
Colors bright, a mystery.
Twists and turns of life's great loom,
Crafting destinies from the gloom.

Each ribbon whispers tales untold,
Of hearts entwined and dreams that unfold.
Paths we take, turns we miss,
In the dance of fate, the sweet abyss.

Loops and knots, a gentle guide,
Through the storms and endless tide.
In every strand, a choice to make,
For loves we nurture, and bonds we break.

Together we weave, together we fray,
In the fabric of life's endless play.
With ribbons of fate, our stories blend,
As we journey on, where dreams ascend.

Whirls of Enchantment

In twilight's hush, the magic brews,
Stars arise, a cosmic muse.
Gentle whirls of night remain,
Where dreams and hopes intertwine like veins.

Dancing lights in silver streams,
Carrying whispers of forgotten dreams.
Each twirl a promise, a secret sigh,
In the embrace of the starlit sky.

With every breath, the world spins round,
In the enchantment, our souls unbound.
Caught in the rhythm of what will be,
A serenade of a wish set free.

Whirls of wonder, linger near,
In the realms where dreams appear.
To the melody of a heart's sweet trance,
We find our fate in the dance's romance.

Tempest of Tomorrow

Clouds gather strong, the winds ignite,
A tempest brews, darkening the light.
Thunder rolls with a fierce lament,
Echoing fears, the past's descent.

Yet in the storm, seeds are sown,
A promise whispered, a chance once known.
From chaos springs a brand new dawn,
With every wreckage, a strength reborn.

Rain falls like tears from skies above,
Washing wounds, a testament of love.
Through swirling gales, we hold our ground,
In the tempest's heart, hope is found.

For tomorrow waits, a canvas bright,
Painted by the storm's fierce fight.
In the aftermath, we rise again,
Embracing life, through loss and pain.

Song of the Cyclones

Whispers dance in tempest's might,
Clouds gather, dark as night.
Winds howl a haunting tune,
Nature's fury, a wild boon.

Branches sway like restless souls,
Lightning flash, thunder rolls.
Raging seas, a boisterous roar,
Cyclones chant, ask for more.

Stormy Adventures

Riders chase the rolling waves,
Over hills, through stormy graves.
Courage brews in hearts of gold,
Storms unfold their tales untold.

Skies crackle with electric flair,
Journey forth, if you dare.
With every gust, spirits rise,
Chasing dreams beneath wild skies.

Edges of the Gale

Winds whisper secrets in the dark,
On the edge, we leave our mark.
Debris swirls in nature's hand,
Together, we will take a stand.

Breathless moments, hearts aligned,
In the storm, true paths combined.
Lost and found in swirling grace,
We embrace this wild space.

Tempestuous Echoes

Echoes roar through valleys steep,
Nature's voice will not let sleep.
Footsteps trace the storm's own beat,
In its arms, we find our seat.

Time unfolds with every blast,
Whirling winds and shadows cast.
In the tempest, dreams ignite,
As stars emerge to greet the night.

Rhapsody in the Eye of the Storm

Amidst the chaos, calm resides,
Whispers of peace in raging tides.
Nature's fury, yet softly sung,
A melody of strength, forever young.

Dancing shadows play on waves,
Lost in the sound that nature saves.
Storms may roar, but tunes endure,
A symphony of wild and pure.

Spiraling Serenades

Notes like feathers drift and glide,
Caught in the winds, they twist with pride.
Each sound a story, spun on air,
Whirling around without a care.

In spirals soft, the music flows,
Echoing where the warm breeze blows.
A dance of dreams, both light and free,
Serenades of what could be.

Chasing Elysium

Across the fields of golden grain,
Footsteps trace a sweet refrain.
In pursuit of joys untold,
Hearts embrace the brave and bold.

With every breath, the spirits rise,
Chasing visions through endless skies.
Elysium calls with gentle grace,
A cherished dream we dare to chase.

Dance of the Sighing Winds

The winds confide in whispered tones,
Carrying tales of ancient stones.
They sway the trees with rhythmic grace,
A dance of time, a broad embrace.

Beneath the boughs, the world stands still,
Nature's heartbeat, calming thrill.
In every sigh, a story bends,
Flowing softly as the day ends.

Swirling Hopes

In the dusk, dreams take flight,
Whispered wishes in the night.
Stars align, a guiding fire,
Hearts aflame with pure desire.

Through the storms, we find our way,
Chasing dawn, the break of day.
Hope will rise like morning dew,
Bringing life to all we do.

Zephyrs of Possibility

Gentle winds caress the trees,
Carrying thoughts like autumn leaves.
Softly spoken, sweet refrain,
Every moment feels the same.

In this dance of sighs and dreams,
Nothing's ever as it seems.
Pulling at the threads of fate,
Letting go, we learn to wait.

Dance of the Dreams

In twilight's glow, shadows play,
Spinning tales of night and day.
Whirling past on starlit scenes,
Life unfolds in vivid dreams.

Every twirl, a wish unspun,
Chasing echoes, one by one.
Ballet of the hearts' delight,
Graceful paths in endless flight.

Storm of Yearning

Clouds gather, a tempest rise,
Whirlwinds hug the heavy skies.
Hearts are tossed, like ships at sea,
Yearning for what's meant to be.

Lightning strikes, the moment calls,
From the depths, our spirit sprawls.
In the chaos, find the peace,
Resilience grows, sweet release.

Spiral of Illusions

In shadows deep, the colors fade,
A dance of dreams, a fleeting trade.
Whispers twist in a silent scream,
Reality breaks, or so it seems.

Echoes laugh in the curtain's fold,
Tales of warmth turn bitterly cold.
Eyes can't see what the heart can find,
A labyrinth spun from a wandering mind.

Whispers in the Wind

Softly spoken, the secrets play,
Carried far where the wild hearts sway.
Glimmers of truth slide between the trees,
Embracing night with a tender breeze.

Echoes drift on the moonlit ground,
In each silent verse, love is found.
Nature hums with a timeless grace,
Inviting all to the sacred space.

Whirl of Serendipity

Chance encounters in the morning light,
A glance exchanged feels perfectly right.
Footsteps cross on the path unknown,
Leading hearts to the seeds they've sown.

In laughter shared, the world expands,
Fate's gentle push guides trembling hands.
Magic weaves through the open day,
In serendipity, we find our way.

Twirl of Wishes

Under starlit skies, dreams take flight,
Spinning softly through the starry night.
Each wish cast like a feathered sigh,
Floating gently, it dares to fly.

In the twirl of hope, hearts embrace,
Finding solace in a warm, safe space.
Together we weave the tales anew,
In the twirl of wishes, me and you.

Spirals of Desire

In whispers soft, we meet our fate,
A dance ignites, as passions wait.
Around we twine, like threads of gold,
In moments stolen, our dreams unfold.

Cascading lights, our hearts align,
In twirling paths, where souls entwine.
A spiral formed, in silent glow,
Desires rise, like tides that flow.

Through shadows cast, we chase the night,
A spark so bright, in fading light.
Each turn we take, a story told,
In spirals deep, where love grows bold.

Beyond the bounds, we taste the thrill,
In fervent spirals, time stands still.
With every pulse, our spirits soar,
As we embrace, forevermore.

Vortex of Longings

In swirling dreams, we lose our way,
A vortex pulls, both night and day.
With every thought, a longing grows,
As whispers call, our spirits close.

Around the void, our hopes unite,
In sacred space, we chase the light.
A spiral deep, of wishes spun,
In vortex realms, we come undone.

The pull so strong, we cannot fight,
In currents bold, we seek the height.
With every glance, our fates combine,
In swirling depths, our hearts entwine.

Through paths unknown, we bravely dive,
In vortex wild, we feel alive.
Together here, our souls shall sing,
In endless yearn, the joy we bring.

Tornado of Aspirations

In fierce winds blow, intentions rise,
A tornado spins beneath the skies.
With swirling thoughts, we forge our dreams,
As hope ignites, in silver beams.

The chaos reigns, yet leads the way,
Through broken paths, we dare to stay.
With every turn, ambitions flare,
In the eye of storms, we learn to care.

Around us whirl, our visions bright,
In passion's grip, we chase the light.
Each fleeting moment, a spark in time,
In tornado's dance, our spirits climb.

Through swirling clouds, we find our peace,
In aspirations bold, our fears release.
Together we stand, no path too wide,
In the heart of storms, we shall abide.

Cyclone of Yearnings

In cyclones deep, our hearts revolve,
With every turn, fresh dreams evolve.
Around we spin, in fervent chase,
In whirlwinds strong, we find our place.

A dance unfolds, with winds that play,
As yearnings twist in bright array.
Through shadows cast, we seek the flame,
In cycles strong, we call our name.

Each gust a promise, a breath anew,
In swirling hopes, we break on through.
With every thrust, our passions surge,
In cyclone's dance, our spirits merge.

Through storms we rise, hand in hand tight,
As yearnings weave in endless flight.
Together spun, we find our home,
In cyclones fierce, no need to roam.

Tempest of Dreams

In the night where shadows wail,
Whispers ride the stormy gale.
Hearts aflame with silent screams,
Guided by the pulse of dreams.

Stars collide in a frantic dance,
Haunted visions cast a glance.
Through the chaos, spirits soar,
Seeking solace on the shore.

Waves of doubt crash on the mind,
Yet the light is still defined.
Through the gale, our paths align,
In the tempest, hearts entwine.

Fleeting moments, fleeting nights,
In the fray, we find our sights.
Dreamers roam in echo's keep,
Lost in the lull of seas so deep.

Ceaseless Currents of Hope

Through the valleys, whispers flow,
Carried forth by winds that glow.
Life's a river, swift and bright,
Guiding every heart toward light.

When the shadows threaten change,
Hope remains a vibrant range.
A beacon through the darkest strife,
In every breath, the spark of life.

Stones may tumble, paths may twist,
Yet we hold on through the mist.
With each wave, we learn to trust,
In the currents, rise we must.

Faith, a vessel, strong and true,
Navigates the skies so blue.
Where the tides of time may sweep,
Hope, our anchor, strong and deep.

Fancies in a Flurry

Whirling whispers, thoughts collide,
In a dance where dreams abide.
Colors burst in fleeting sight,
Painted skies in bold delight.

Fluttering wings of fleeting joy,
Childlike visions to enjoy.
Moments twirl in playful glee,
Lost in sweet reverie.

Tangled dreams and vibrant hues,
Each one whispers gentle clues.
Fancies drift like autumn leaves,
Carried forth on magic eves.

In this flurry, we remain,
Chasing echoes like a train.
For in the chaos, we shall find,
The treasures held within the mind.

Cyclone of Longings

In the heart, a tempest swells,
Yearning for what time compels.
Desires swirl like autumn winds,
Racing towards the journey's ends.

Silent echoes stir the soul,
Dreams of love that make us whole.
Through the storm, we reach for grace,
In the cyclone, we find our place.

Turbulence of thoughts unfurled,
Longings dance within this world.
In the eye, a moment's peace,
From the chaos, sweet release.

Every longing tells a tale,
In the winds, we will not pale.
For the heart that dares to fight,
Finds its home in love's pure light.

Tornado of Tomorrow

Spinning dreams in swirling skies,
Hope and chaos intertwine.
The winds of change begin to rise,
Leading us to paths divine.

With every twist and every turn,
Lessons learned and bridges crossed.
In the fury, hearts will yearn,
For the calm, not for the lost.

From the tempest, we emerge,
Strengthened by the wild embrace.
Through the whirlwind, we converge,
Toward the bright and open space.

In the eye, a moment's peace,
A chance to breathe, to redefine.
As the raging winds will cease,
Tomorrow's light, a hopeful sign.

Whispers in the Storm

Gentle words on raging air,
Secrets held in thunder's roar.
Nature speaks, a voice laid bare,
In the darkness, whispers soar.

Clouds encircle, shadows creep,
Tales from ages long ago.
In the silence, silence deep,
Here in chaos, truths will flow.

Glimmers shine through raindrops' fall,
Messages that hearts can feel.
In the clash, we hear the call,
In the storm, we find the real.

Every storm brings forth a shade,
Of the whispers we've ignored.
In the midst, our fears are laid,
Yet the light will be restored.

Gale of Aspirations

Feel the breeze, it stirs the soul,
A gale that lifts our hopes on high.
Through the rush, we seek our goal,
Boundless dreams from earth to sky.

A gust of faith against the strife,
Pushing us to break the mold.
With each breath, we chase our life,
In the winds, our stories told.

As we sail on future's crest,
Oceans wide and skies so blue,
In the tempest, we find rest,
Strengthen hearts with every view.

Harnessing the storm's delight,
With courage woven in our seams.
In the gale, we find our might,
Turn our visions into dreams.

Twirl of the Heart

Dance beneath the silver moon,
Whirls of love in perfect time.
In the dusk, our spirits swoon,
Coupled dreams, a gentle rhyme.

With each spin, we start anew,
Embracing all that life can bring.
In the twirl, my heart finds you,
Love's sweet echo, vibrant fling.

As the stars align above,
Guiding us with softest light.
Every twirl speaks of our love,
In the shadows, hearts take flight.

Through the laughter and the tears,
In the rhythm, we belong.
With each twirl, we'll face our fears,
Together, we are ever strong.

Sighs in the Breeze

Gentle whispers brush the trees,
As daylight fades into the ease.
The sun dips low, a golden tease,
While shadows dance with soft decrees.

Leaves murmur tales from days gone by,
Carried softly on wings that fly.
In this moment, hearts comply,
And every dream begins to sigh.

Clouds parade in twilight's glow,
Painting skies with hues that flow.
The night encroaches, soft and slow,
Embracing all, both fast and low.

With every gust, a secret's spun,
As laughter fades and dreams all run.
In silent corners, thoughts are won,
In sighs, eternal, we become one.

Rushing Thoughts

Whirlwinds churn within the mind,
Ideas spark, leave fears behind.
Memories dance, so intertwined,
In a race where truth is blind.

Questions rise like waves of foam,
Nurturing seeds we've yet to comb.
Searching endless paths to roam,
Chasing echoes of our home.

Fleeting moments fade away,
Leaving traces of yesterday.
Time's a thief that comes to play,
As rushing thoughts begin to sway.

In this storm of silent screams,
We redefine our fleeting dreams.
With every pulse, the spirit beams,
Embracing all that life redeems.

Cyclone of Enchantment

Spirits dance in swirling light,
Colors burst, a wondrous sight.
In this tempest, hearts take flight,
As shadows blend with pure delight.

Whispers weave through the vibrant air,
Crafting spells beyond compare.
With every twirl, we're bound to dare,
In magic's grip, we shed our care.

Swirls of laughter fill the night,
As stars above flicker bright.
From depths of soul, a wild rite,
We find our truth in sheer delight.

Caught in this cyclone, lose the thread,
Of worries left, unspoken dread.
We stand as one, the brave, the fed,
In enchantment's arms, our spirits spread.

Whirl of Potential

In the chaos, seeds we sow,
Hopes aloft, like petals blow.
The future glows, a vibrant show,
In every heart, the dreams we know.

Moments shift, and paths unwind,
With every chance, our fates aligned.
Unseen trails that fate has signed,
In whispers where the stars have shined.

From stagnant pools, new currents rise,
Eager leaps toward open skies.
With every breath, the spirit flies,
In the whirlwind, we find our ties.

So let us dance in endless spin,
For every loss, there's found within,
A world of light that's set to win,
In the whirl of potential, we begin.

Aspirations in the Storm

In the heart of the tempest, we rise,
Daring to chase the ever-dark skies.
With grit that ignites in the howl of despair,
We stand in the rain, with dreams laid bare.

Each drop a reminder of hopes we hold tight,
Facing the furious winds, igniting our flight.
The thunder may roar, but we won't back down,
With courage our armor, we claim our crown.

The waves may crash, yet we forge our way,
Uttering promises in the storm's cruel sway.
A spark of ambition in chaos unfurled,
Together we navigate this turbulent world.

So as shadows linger and doubts seem grand,
We plant our feet firm on this shifting sand.
For aspirations bloom even in the strife,
Guided by dreams that lead to new life.

Cyclone of Serenity

In the eye of the cyclone, we find our peace,
A stillness surrounding, where worries cease.
Whispers of calm in a high-stakes dance,
We breathe in the moment, embracing the chance.

Through swirling chaos, our spirits remain,
Riding the breezes that flow like a train.
With each gentle gust, our spirits take flight,
Finding the beauty in the midst of the night.

We gather the strength from the winds that we hear,
Transforming the turmoil into something clear.
For in the bluster, a soft voice does shout,
Reminding us gently what life's all about.

So let us not fear the tempest outside,
But find our own rhythm, our inner guide.
In storms we discover serenity's song,
A cyclone of stillness where we all belong.

Windswept Dreams

Beneath the wide heavens, our visions take flight,
Carried on breezes, both gentle and light.
We clutch at the hopes that the sky has to share,
Windswept and wild, we embrace the dare.

In the dance of the zephyrs, our wishes unfold,
Stories of future in whispers retold.
Every breath draws us closer to what we aspire,
Inflated with passion and endless desire.

Through valleys and mountains, our dreams soar above,
Guided by starlight, they shine like a dove.
With winds as our compass, we chase the unknown,
With hearts intertwined, we're never alone.

For dreams are the feathers that float on the breeze,
They tell of the journeys that sweep through the trees.
In the arms of the wind, our spirits are free,
Windswept and bold, we become what we see.

Flight of the Aspirations

With wings made of hope, we ascend to the skies,
Each flap of our heart echoes daring goodbyes.
We leave behind doubts, like shadows they fade,
Chasing the visions that life has displayed.

In the warmth of our dreams, we drift ever high,
Soaring through clouds where aspirations lie.
Each gust of ambition propels us along,
In the assembly of dreams, we find our strong song.

Navigating storms with a courage anew,
Our passion the fuel, forever in view.
For flight is the canvas where wishes take form,
A dance in the sky where our spirits are warm.

So rise up together, let's chase the sun bright,
In the story of dreams, we'll take our own flight.
With every horizon, our journey extends,
In the arms of the skies, our passion transcends.

Wild Flight of Imagination

In the sky of dreams, we soar,
Beyond the clouds, forevermore.
Colors swirl in endless dance,
Taking wings, we find our chance.

Whispers of thoughts on breezes glide,
Painting worlds where hopes abide.
A canvas stretched by endless light,
Our spirits free, in pure delight.

Through valleys deep, and mountains high,
We chase the visions that never die.
With every heartbeat, stories weave,
In the wild flight, we believe.

Flurry of Hopes and Dreams

In a flurry of whispers, hopes arise,
Carried gently beneath soft skies.
Hearts aflame with a vibrant glow,
Each dream a seed we long to sow.

A dance of wishes, like swirling snow,
Fleeting moments in the afterglow.
We cast our lanterns into the night,
Guided by visions, we chase the light.

With every step, the path unfolds,
In the mosaic of life, our stories told.
A symphony of desires on the breeze,
In the flurry, we find our peace.

Roar of the Aspirational Winds

The winds of change begin to howl,
Whispers grow into a mighty prowl.
Voices rise, a powerful chord,
With every breath, we seek reward.

Through forests deep where shadows play,
We chase the dreams that light the way.
An echo strong, a call to rise,
In the roar, we claim the skies.

Hope unfurls like sails at sea,
A journey bright with destiny.
Together we stand, as hearts align,
In the winds, our futures shine.

Driftwood of Desire

On the shore where dreams collide,
The driftwood tells tales of the tide.
Worn and weathered, yet so bold,
In its curves, our hopes unfold.

Tides of yearning wash ashore,
Carving paths to forevermore.
Each splintered piece a story grand,
In driftwood's embrace, we take our stand.

As the waves dance under the sun,
We gather wishes, one by one.
In the ocean's arms, we find our way,
With driftwood desires, we boldly sway.

Tornado of Beliefs

In the heart of the storm, truth swirls,
A dance of thoughts, where chaos unfurls.
Whispers of doubt, like debris in flight,
Tearing through silence, obscuring the light.

Roots of conviction shake in the gale,
Each belief tested, some rise, some fail.
But amidst the ruins, new visions can bloom,
A promising dawn after nights spent in gloom.

The spiral of strength, both fierce and profound,
In every tempest, our voices resound.
Tornado of beliefs, shows what we choose,
In the eye of the storm, we find hope to use.

Cyclonic Visions

Swirling like colors in an artist's hand,
Dreams take flight, unbound by the land.
Vivid and wild, they twist and they turn,
In the heart of the storm, new passions burn.

Glimmers of futures, so bright yet so far,
Caught in the chaos, they flicker like stars.
The winds of change whisper soft in the night,
Guiding our souls with their ethereal light.

A cyclone of thoughts, relentless and free,
Riding the waves of what's meant to be.
Cyclonic visions spin dreams into view,
Painting the skies in each vibrant hue.

Breezes of Change

Gentle whispers that dance through the trees,
Carrying secrets upon a soft breeze.
Change comes softly, like dawn's early light,
Transforming the world from dark into bright.

Each leaf that rustles, each petal that falls,
Echoes the promise of nature's own calls.
Embracing the shift, we learn to let go,
Breezes of change guide where we need to flow.

In stillness we find the strength to renew,
Drawing from roots that steady and true.
Breezes of change, we welcome with grace,
They mold our path, we find our place.

Gale of Desires

A fierce wind howls, awakening dreams,
The gale of desires, bursting at seams.
Passions ignited, like stars in the night,
Driving the heart towards limitless height.

With every strong gust, our spirits are bold,
Chasing the visions that spark in our soul.
Each wish a sail, catching currents unseen,
In the storm of our yearnings, we strive to glean.

Through struggles and trials, we learn to endure,
The gale of desires makes us more sure.
So let the winds carry what's deeply desired,
For in every tempest, our hearts are inspired.

Flows of Fancy

In a world of dreams we glide,
Where whispers of the heart reside.
Colors dance in gentle waves,
Carrying thoughts that the spirit saves.

Beneath the soft and glowing light,
Imagination takes its flight.
Through the fields of flora bright,
Crafting visions in the night.

Every note, a fleeting sound,
In the silence, beauty found.
With every step, we weave the lore,
Of floating dreams that we adore.

Bated Breaths in the Gale

The wind whispers secrets gray,
As clouds above begin to sway.
Heartbeats quicken with the storm,
In this wild, electric form.

Gusts that dance through twisted trees,
Carry hopes on fleeting breeze.
Each sigh bends the world in time,
With nature's pulse, all thoughts align.

Amid the chaos, calm awaits,
The world transforms; the heart debates.
To find solace in the strife,
In fateful breaths, we find our life.

Reverberations of Hope

In shadows deep, a light will gleam,
A flicker born from every dream.
The echoes of tomorrow's call,
Encourage all who fear to fall.

With open arms, the dawn will break,
As fragile hearts begin to wake.
Each pulse a beat of faith restored,
In unity, our spirits soared.

The melodies of worlds collide,
Cradled in the arms of tide.
Together we will stand and cope,
Unyielding bonds of endless hope.

Twists of Destiny

Paths untraveled lay ahead,
With choices veiled, and futures spread.
Each turn a test, a chance to grow,
In life's embrace, we learn to flow.

Moments shifting, bringing change,
In the journey, we rearrange.
With every step, the story bends,
As old beginnings find their ends.

Threads of fate, entwined we weave,
With every breath, we dare believe.
In the tapestry of time, we find,
The beauty born from the intertwined.

Tidal Surge of Dreams

Waves of thought crash ashore,
Carrying whispers of lore.
Drifting hopes on the tide,
In the depths, dreams reside.

Moonlit paths draw near,
Guiding through night's sheer.
Shores of desire extend,
Where lost wishes mend.

A swell of vibrant light,
Beckons with pure delight.
Fragments of futures bright,
Rising high in the night.

Embrace the current's flow,
Let the inner heart grow.
In the sea of the mind,
All the treasures we find.

Spin of Spirited Wishes

In the dance of the breeze,
Dreams twirl like autumn leaves.
Flickering wishes ignite,
Creating warmth from the light.

Stars align in a night sky,
Guiding hearts that dare fly.
Spirals of hope take a leap,
In the silence, we keep.

Roots entwined in the ground,
In each heartbeat, they're found.
Invisible threads connect,
Each wish a soft whisper to respect.

Together we weave our fate,
On the wheel of love, don't wait.
Spin your dreams, let them soar,
In the wind, forevermore.

Euphoria in the Eye of Chaos

In the storm, there's a calm,
A sweet touch, a gentle balm.
Through the darkness, we see,
The light that sets us free.

Chaos dances, wild and bright,
Yet we find strength in the fight.
Whirling in the tempest's sigh,
Euphoria as we fly.

Eyes wide open to the fear,
In the swirl, we find cheer.
Moments spun in delight,
Guide us through the night.

Hold tight to the fleeting grace,
In each challenge, find your place.
For in turmoil's embrace,
Love shines with a warm face.

Tornado of the Soul's Fantasies

Spirals twist in our mind,
Whirling dreams intertwined.
Carried on winds of thought,
Fantasies boldly sought.

The center holds a bright light,
Illuminating the night.
Voices swirl in the whine,
Merging with the divine.

In this dance of the heart,
Every piece plays its part.
A cyclone of pure desire,
Igniting our spirit's fire.

Caught in this vivid storm,
Find your truth and transform.
For in chaos, we discover,
The beauty of one another.

Vortex of the Heart

In the depths where feelings roam,
Whispers twirl in shadows' dome.
Tornadoes spin of love and pain,
Tugging gently at the chain.

Chasing hopes that rise and fall,
Echoes dance within the hall.
Round and round, emotions steep,
Binding dreams that dare to leap.

Twisting paths of fate align,
Merging souls, your heart in mine.
Through the storm, we find our way,
In the vortex, we shall stay.

Swirl of Daring Thoughts

In the mind where ideas spin,
Daring visions draw us in.
Spirals of creativity,
Unfolding bright, a tapestry.

Whirling dreams on whispers' wing,
Challenging what the heart might bring.
Thoughts entwined, a bold embrace,
In the swirl, we find our place.

Fleeting sparks ignite the night,
In this dance, we feel the light.
Allow the currents to take flight,
In daring thoughts, we shine so bright.

Breeze of Unspoken Yearnings

Softly blow the silent pleas,
Through the branches of the trees.
Gentle gusts of dreams unsaid,
Carried where the heart has led.

Hidden hopes in every sigh,
Wandering stars that fill the sky.
Fleeting moments, whispers sweet,
In this breeze, our souls will meet.

Drifting closer, tenderly,
Like the waves upon the sea.
Unveiling all the thoughts we hide,
In the breeze, our hearts confide.

Cascade of Bright Possibilities

From the mountain, visions flow,
Rushing forth, a vibrant show.
Each drop sparkles with a dream,
In the light, life's flowing stream.

Choices tumble, wild and free,
Carving paths through destiny.
A cascade of hopeful hues,
Every splash, a chance to choose.

Shimmering in the morning sun,
The journey waits for everyone.
Dive right in, let go of fears,
In this cascade, laughter cheers.

Whirls of Possibility

In the dance of dreams we twirl,
Where hopes alight and visions swirl.
Every choice a path we take,
In shadows deep, our futures wake.

Around us worlds begin to form,
In chaos lies the heart's true storm.
With every step, new chances rise,
A symphony beneath the skies.

Moments shimmer, brightly spun,
With every breath, a chance begun.
In whirls of thought, we chase the light,
Unlocking realms that feel so right.

So leap into the vast unknown,
With wings of courage, love has grown.
In whirls of possibility, we find,
A treasure trove of heart and mind.

Fires in the Storm

Beneath the clouds, a flicker glows,
A fire born where wild wind blows.
In tempest's howl, our spirits soar,
Through raging storms, we seek for more.

The lightning strikes, a spark ignites,
A warmth that burns in darkest nights.
In chaos, passion finds its form,
Through swirling skies, we brave the storm.

Embers dance on fleeting breath,
In every moment, life and death.
We rise anew from ashes gray,
With fires that guide us on our way.

Through thunder's roar, our hearts collide,
In storms where fierce desires reside.
With fires in the storm, we blaze,
In every shadow, love's bright praise.

Gales of Passion

Winds sweep in with fierce embrace,
Carrying the breath of grace.
In gales that twist and turn the night,
Our souls ignite, a vibrant light.

With every gust, the heart takes flight,
In wild abandon, we unite.
Through swirling air, our spirits race,
In passion's grip, we find our place.

The world may spin, a tempest's art,
Yet in this storm, we play our part.
With every shout, we claim the skies,
In gales of passion, love defies.

So let the wind blow fierce and free,
For in its strength, it's you and me.
Together, we will brave the storm,
In gales of passion, hearts stay warm.

Chasing Tornadoes

Across the plains, the skies grow dark,
A swirling dance, we feel the spark.
With hearts ablaze, we chase the fierce,
Through raging winds, our souls immerse.

The funnel spins, a deadly grace,
In nature's fury, we find our place.
In every twist, a thrill unfolds,
Chasing tornadoes, brave and bold.

The tempest calls, a wild song,
Where echoes of the brave belong.
We run towards the swirling might,
In storms that dare us through the night.

Fueled by dreams and fierce delight,
We chase the winds that twist in flight.
For in the storm, we find our way,
Chasing tornadoes, come what may.

Enchanted by the Breeze

Whispers of wind through the trees,
Carrying tales on a gentle tease.
Petals dance lightly, a sweet embrace,
Nature's soft breath, a tranquil space.

Sun-kissed moments pass by so fast,
A fleeting spell, a memory cast.
Dreams drift like clouds in the sky's expanse,
In the heart's rhythm, we find romance.

Echoes of laughter, the world's refrain,
Woven with sunlight, free from pain.
Every sigh in the air feels alive,
In this magic, we learn to thrive.

In the dawn's glow, all worries cease,
Wrapped in the solace of purest peace.
With every breath, let the spirit roam,
In the breeze's dance, we find our home.

Whirl of the Mind's Desires

Thoughts collide like stars in the night,
Spinning in circles, taking flight.
Fleeting visions, bold and bright,
Craving the dreams that spark delight.

Whispers of hope in shadows cast,
Yearning for moments that forever last.
In every heartbeat, a secret confide,
Chasing the feelings we try to hide.

The canvas of life, splashed with our yearn,
In each brushstroke, our passions burn.
As the heart races, and spirits soar,
Embrace the madness, seek to explore.

In the dance of wishes, we find our truth,
Fueling the flames of ageless youth.
Let desires lead in this swirling spree,
In the whirl of the mind, we are set free.

Flight of Fancy

Wings of imagination spread wide,
Soaring above the timid tide.
Clouds become castles, dreams take flight,
In a world where everything feels right.

Glimmers of magic linger in air,
Every heartbeat a spark, a flare.
With each breath, the limits break,
Into a realm where we can awake.

Across the horizon, horizons expand,
Nothing but wonder at our command.
Ideas like arrows shot with grace,
In the sky's embrace, we find our place.

Dancing on whispers of hope's sweet song,
In this adventure, we all belong.
Let the fantasy guide, let it lead,
In the flight of fancy, we plant the seed.

Fluttering Intentions

Delicate dreams take wing and sway,
In the soft glow of the breaking day.
Hearts flutter gently on whispers of fate,
As we gather courage and contemplate.

Intentions formed like butterflies bright,
Emerging from shadows, craving the light.
In every flutter, a story unfolds,
A tapestry spun with brave hearts bold.

Moments of stillness, where feelings bloom,
Nurtured with hope, dispelling the gloom.
With every whisper, intentions ignite,
In the dance of the heart, we feel the light.

So let us chase dreams with grace anew,
Embracing the wonder in all that we do.
In the fluttering dance of life's endless flow,
Intentions take flight, like seeds we sow.

Echoes of Aspirations

In shadows of dreams, we wander free,
Chasing the light where our hopes can be.
Whispers of past dance in our ears,
Fueling our souls, melting our fears.

Each step we take, a story unfolds,
Mountains of courage, we dare to hold.
Voices of promise, ringing so true,
Brightening paths that were once askew.

The road may twist, the journey is long,
Yet in our hearts, we share the song.
Embers ignite from the spark of will,
Echoes of aspirations, soaring still.

Whirl of Zephyrs

Gentle the breeze that brushes our skin,
Softly it beckons, pulling us in.
Through trees it flutters, a lively dance,
Carrying whispers of sweet romance.

Golden the sun on a clear azure,
Painting the sky, its hues so pure.
Zephyrs entwine in a joyous spin,
Nature's own hymn, where dreams begin.

Each gust a promise, each swirl a kiss,
In the embrace of this tranquil bliss.
We sway and surrender to nature's grace,
Lost in the moment, a warm embrace.

Vortex of Bliss

In the heart of the storm, we find our peace,
Where worries dissolve and sorrows cease.
Spinning in circles, we rise and we fall,
Wrapped in the warmth, we heed the call.

Colors collide in a vibrant hue,
Crafting a canvas, both bold and true.
Here in the center, the chaos aligns,
A whirlwind of joy, in perfect designs.

Each breath a rhythm, each heartbeat a song,
In this vortex of bliss, we know we belong.
Dancing through moments, both fleeting and bright,
Finding our way in the softest light.

Dancing Among the Winds

With arms wide open, we twirl and glide,
Carried by currents, nowhere to hide.
The winds sing a tune, so wild and free,
Inviting our spirits to follow the spree.

Through fields of daisies, we spin and sway,
Chasing the clouds on a breezy day.
Laughter and whispers weave tales in the air,
A dance of togetherness, free from care.

The evening descends, with stars shining bright,
We celebrate life, in the cool of the night.
Amongst the winds, our hearts intertwine,
United in rhythm, a love so divine.

Currents of the Heart's Yearning

In the silence of the night, we sigh,
Waves of longing drift and fly.
Stars above twinkle like dreams,
Carried softly on moonlit beams.

Whispers call from the distant shore,
Echoes of love we can't ignore.
Hearts entangled, lost in time,
Seeking solace in love's sweet rhyme.

Cyclonic Whispers of Fate

A tempest stirs where shadows creep,
Fate's whispers tug, and secrets seep.
The winds of change begin to howl,
As destiny dons its stormy cowl.

In swirling chaos, choices clash,
Moments fleeting, life a flash.
Through the storm, we learn to stand,
Guided by fate's unseen hand.

Gusts of Hope

Amidst the clouds, a bright light glows,
Hope arises, chance bestows.
Softly blowing, it stirs the soul,
Gusts of change make broken whole.

In every heart, a fire ignites,
Fueling dreams, chasing heights.
Together we soar, a steadfast team,
Riding high on hope's warm beam.

Dreams in the Tempest

Beneath the storm, our dreams take flight,
Casting shadows, embracing light.
Tenacious hearts, unyielding and bold,
Navigate the chaos, their stories told.

With every wave that crashes near,
We rise anew, conquering fear.
In the heart of the raging storm,
Dreams bloom bright, steadfast and warm.

Windblown Wishes

In the quiet of the night,
Whispers drift on the breeze,
Carrying hopes and dreams,
Dancing through the trees.

Stars twinkle in the dark,
Lighting paths we can't see,
Each wish a glowing spark,
Floating wild and free.

With every gust that sighs,
Secrets swirl in the air,
A chorus of soft cries,
For the brave and the rare.

As dawn ushers in light,
Wishes fly out of sight,
Yet they linger in our hearts,
Boundless journeys, new starts.

Stormy Serenade

Thunder rolls in the night,
A symphony of dark,
Raindrops fall, pure delight,
Nature's vibrant arc.

Lightning dances on high,
Illuminating the sky,
Each flash a fleeting dream,
As shadows swirl and scream.

Wind howls through the trees,
A haunting, wild song,
Nature sways in the breeze,
Where all souls belong.

In the heart of the storm,
We find chaos and peace,
A world reborn, transformed,
In the tempest's release.

Twirl of Fantasies

In a land of golden hues,
Where the flowers freely sway,
Dreams take flight like butterflies,
In the light of the day.

Spinning stories in the wind,
Colors blend, a sweet surprise,
Every twirl a brand new hope,
Beneath the endless skies.

With laughter riding high,
We twirl in pure delight,
Each moment a gentle sigh,
As whispers fill the night.

Memories weave and dance,
In the heart's embrace we stay,
Lost in this sweet romance,
Forever swept away.

Maelstrom of Dreams

In the depths of the night,
Dreams swirl like a storm,
Caught in a cosmic flight,
Where visions transform.

Fleeting moments collide,
In a chaos of grace,
Waves of wonder abide,
In this surreal space.

Through shadows and light,
We chase what may be real,
A thrilling, endless flight,
There's so much to feel.

From whispers, we create,
A tapestry of hope,
In the whirlwinds, we wait,
For the chance to elope.

Circles of Ambition

In shadows cast by lofty dreams,
We chase the light of silver beams.
With every step, the world expands,
Yet fragile as the finest sands.

A ladder built of whispered wishes,
Each rung a spark, each breath, our riches.
The echoes of our fervent calls,
Ring out through grand and gilded halls.

In fervid flames, our passions burn,
Through trials faced, we strive, we learn.
The compass points to skies anew,
As we embark, our visions true.

Together, hand in hand we soar,
Through open fields, to distant shore.
With every heartbeat, we create,
Our destinies, a twist of fate.

Uproar of Hopes

In whispers loud, our dreams take flight,
Across the canvas, day and night.
They paint the sky with vibrant hues,
A symphony of endless views.

From fractured pasts to futures bright,
We gather strength from darkest plight.
A chorus rises, hearts ablaze,
Together we will dare, we'll raise.

With every dawn, new chances found,
In unity, we stand our ground.
The chorus swells, our spirits blend,
With every note, we shall ascend.

Emboldened by this fervent call,
We rise as giants, never small.
Through every trial, we ignite,
The uproar of our hopes, so bright.

Dreaming in the Breeze

The gentle winds, they call my name,
In softest whispers, play their game.
I close my eyes, the world drifts by,
As dreams take root and start to fly.

Beneath the skies, where wildflowers sway,
I find the peace to float away.
Each breath a chance to let life flow,
In breezes warm, new seeds we sow.

The sunlight dances on my skin,
A fleeting glance, where I begin.
I'm lost in thoughts that intertwine,
As nature cradles all that's mine.

In every rustle, stories weave,
Of hopes and wishes that we believe.
I'll chase the dreams that fill the air,
And trust the breeze will take me there.

Tempest of the Heart

In stormy skies, the thunder roars,
The heart erupts, as silence soars.
With every clash, confusion reigns,
A symphony of love and pains.

Yet through the chaos, sparks ignite,
The fierce desire to hold on tight.
For in the dark, the stars will guide,
Through tempest trails, where dreams abide.

With every wave, the dancing tide,
Will carry hopes, as fears subside.
Our hearts are ships in wild embrace,
Navigating through this wretched space.

When turbulence brings shadows near,
We'll find the strength to face our fear.
And in this storm, we'll play our part,
Resilient souls, a tempest heart.

Twirls of Hope

In the morning light we rise,
Whispers of dreams fill the skies.
Dancing shadows, soft and bright,
Twirls of hope in our sight.

With every step, we chase the dawn,
Beneath the trees, the world is drawn.
Leaves flutter gently, hearts will soar,
Twirls of hope, forevermore.

Through trials faced, we stand as one,
Together, we shine like the sun.
In every laugh, in every tear,
Twirls of hope shall persevere.

So let us sing, let spirits free,
In unity, we'll always be.
A journey bright, though paths may slope,
In our hearts, we weave our hope.

Reveries in the Gales

Amidst the whispers of the breeze,
We lose ourselves among the trees.
Memories swirl, both far and near,
Reveries in the gales we hear.

Each note of laughter, a distant chime,
Tales of old, woven in rhyme.
The winds carry stories untold,
Reveries, like dreams of gold.

With every gust, our spirits dance,
In nature's arms, we find romance.
Echoing softly, sweet and clear,
Reveries in the gales appear.

So let us wander, let us roam,
In this embrace, we find our home.
The world spins wild, but we shall stay,
In reveries, we'll find our way.

Flourish Among the Tempests

When storms arise and clouds grow dark,
We stand together, hearts a spark.
In chaos fierce, we find our ground,
Flourish among the tempests found.

With courage firm, we face the night,
Unyielding hearts, a brilliant light.
Through thunder's roar and lightning's flash,
Flourish among the tempests' clash.

Each drop of rain, a lesson learned,
In wildness, wisdom's flame is burned.
Together strong, we brave the ride,
Flourish through storms side by side.

So let the winds howl and winds bend,
In unity, our spirits mend.
For in the heart where courage hums,
We flourish as the tempest comes.

Rhapsody of Wishes

In the twilight glow, we send our dreams,
Flowing softly like silver streams.
With every heartbeat, wishes arise,
A rhapsody painted across the skies.

Each star that twinkles, a longing shared,
In whispered hopes, we are declared.
Boundless joys, like fireflies,
A rhapsody of wishes flies.

From depths of hearts, the melodies swell,
In harmony, together we dwell.
With hope's embrace, we shall not part,
A rhapsody woven through every heart.

So let the night carry our song,
In this symphony where we belong.
For in each wish, our dreams will rise,
A rhapsody beneath the stars' guise.

Chasing the Winds

Across the fields we run, so free,
With laughter echoing, wild reverie.
The breeze whispers secrets, soft and light,
Chasing the winds, we ignite the night.

Leaves twirl around in a playful spin,
A dance with the spirits, where dreams begin.
We twine with the air, our hearts in flight,
Chasing the winds, in pure delight.

Clouds drift above, a canvas so bright,
Painting our stories, from day to night.
With every gust, our hopes take wing,
Chasing the winds, where freedom sings.

Hand in hand, we embrace the day,
With nature's rhythm, we'll find our way.
In every storm, we'll hold on tight,
Chasing the winds, our spirits ignite.

Whipping Up Dreams

In a quiet corner where wishes dwell,
We conjure the magic, a whispered spell.
With each flicker of hope, we soar above,
Whipping up dreams, alight with love.

Beneath the starlit sky, we take our chance,
To dance with the visions, in a mystic trance.
Every heartbeat a promise, bold and bright,
Whipping up dreams, we ignite the night.

Threads of our desires, woven with care,
Filling the air with laughter to share.
Together we rise, like birds in a flight,
Whipping up dreams, a glorious sight.

With eyes wide open, we chase the dawn,
Painting our futures, a vision drawn.
In fields of wonder, our dreams take flight,
Whipping up dreams, pure and right.

A Whirl of Magenta

Petals dance in the evening air,
Swirling colors, a canvas rare.
Magenta hues paint the twilight sky,
A whirl of magenta as the night draws nigh.

From blossoms blooming, whispers arise,
In every color, a world of surprise.
Hearts intertwined, we let our souls play,
A whirl of magenta at the end of the day.

With every twirl, our spirits collide,
Lost in the magic, we laugh and glide.
Painting our dreams in vibrant display,
A whirl of magenta, come what may.

As shadows lengthen, stars start to gleam,
We chase the colors, lost in a dream.
In this blissful dance, we find our way,
A whirl of magenta, forever to stay.

Dance of the Tempest

Thunder rolls like a wild drumbeat,
As lightning flashes, chaos and heat.
Nature's fury, a powerful force,
The dance of the tempest, a raging course.

Winds howl fiercely, a primal scream,
Dark clouds gather, a harrowing theme.
Yet in the storm, our hearts take flight,
The dance of the tempest, fierce and bright.

In the eye of the storm, peace finds its way,
A moment of calm before the melee.
We twirl with the shadows, fearless and bold,
The dance of the tempest, a story told.

Through the rain and the roar, we find our might,
In nature's embrace, we own the night.
With each thunderclap, we rise and sway,
The dance of the tempest, come what may.